CW01456375

AVEBURY

Shearsman Library Vol. 5

ALSO BY RICHARD BERENGARTEN

SELECTED WRITINGS *

OTHER POETRY

PROSE

AS EDITOR

* Published by Shearsman Books

Richard Berengarten

AVEBURY

Shearsman Library

Second Edition.
Published in the United Kingdom in 2018 by
Shearsman Library
an imprint of Shearsman Books
by Shearsman Books Ltd
50 Westons Hill Drive
Emersons Green
BRISTOL
BS16 7DF

Shearsman Books Ltd Registered Office
30–31 St. James Place, Mangotsfield, Bristol BS16 9JB
(this address not for correspondence)

www.shearsman.com

ISBN 978-1-84861-589-2

First published by Anvil Press Poetry
& Routledge Kegan Paul, London, 1972,
and subsequently collected in the author's
For the Living: Selected Longer Poems 1965-2000.

Copyright © Richard Burns, 1972
All rights reserved

The right of Richard Berengarten (Richard Burns) to be identified
as the author of this work has been asserted by him in accordance
with Section 77 of the Copyright, Designs and Patents Act 1988.

*Cover & title page: 'Avebury Standing Stone'
copyright © ian35mm, via istockphoto.com*

Flyleaf: map of Avebury, ca. 1773.

for Octavio Paz

To rise up and become wakeful guardians of the living and of the dead.

HERAKLEITOS OF EPHESUS

And the Lord shall be King over all the earth; in that day shall the Lord be One and his Name One.

SABBATH MORNING SERVICE

For the first time in our history we are contemporaries of all mankind.

OCTAVIO PAZ

huge slabs
wrenched
from under grass, dug
out of hills

time's
teeth

worn

yawning the sky in

porte of light

earthed

tongued

broken
altars

answerless

covered the cave's
cracked jaw

[2]

back and forth
    round and round
under the cloudy dome speechless

sniffing among these petrified hopes
    these ossified dreams   these
    dead memorials   pacing
    back and forth

  ancestorless

under the compact slogans of the sky

        walking
        as dead

  cursing
    their answers
    their meaning

looking for what

        the riddle ?
        the question ?

[3]

and can the stone know
me   I wonder
  does the stone
        wonder

even here   among absences
and wreckage

   if any place

[4]

if any place
most of all

here, most
of any

in the dance
in the ring
of stones dancing
metaphor on metaphor
silence
anagrammatized
measured   spaced out
in this syntax of land
this plot of time

where the green causeway ends
where the avenue ends
where thought ends

begins
the burial
the dance
of stone
begins

[5]

the sky's throat
says

Ascend Sun

from this syntax of hills
        this plot of space

                    mean

            light

        ripples
expanding
        across the downs
                    waves returning
    from where ? the centre
to where ? circumference

            now any
            place is now

                say the stones

I do not tell   I say

little mother
of Willendorf
     'vegetable' Venus
of the hunters
     neckless head
featureless
     under the beehive hair
thin arms asleep   on breasts
     like hills   belly
     enormous   the buttocks
steatopygous   the whole blind body
     bowed over the womb
as if above
     an unseen child

[7]

in the gallery
contorted   struggling
The Prisoners
one in limbs and torse
          nigh perfect, yet
with genitals
          trapped
under unhewn rock
          the arms
          unable to heave
backbreaking
          stone off his head
undiscovered
          dreaming in

and at Samothraki
striding out   came dancing
    Nike
    the daughter

      headless
in the wind   and taking wings
    her robe a river of hair
over the jutting curve of her
      incredible arrogant breasts

    and the breakers
      confluent
   under the belly
    forming   like an unseen hand
protecting her cave   the mouth of her

[9]

on snake island
two *phalloi*
   unsheathed from stone like flowers
      and the air parched
                  so high above the sea
that time of year, August
            with *Meltemi* blowing
   and an hour by boat back to Mykonos

                  poised erect
                     twin offerings
               twin motives

   one of the shafts
broken
   above the marble scrotum

[10]

now see where in marble play
            the musicians: a sturdy
flautist with double pipes
                        stuck in his chinless face
his companion seated at a cracked harp

    nameless the song   from a cave by the sea

                    silence

            still growing
            out of,   louder

    heads uptilted   blinded by sunlight

            the tune climbing, still
            going strong in

    great dusky sea, so many pebbles round your neck
    so many glinting jewels in your hair

[11]

I am awake
sleeping, I wake

in
the cave, tomb
    and temple

            under
    turrets that wind
        and climb

            deep in your chambers

where I lost my memory
            of concerns and imports
                and the way
                up is way
                down

    of all but boyhood

            those dead children

        ghosts

I said
I never believed in

            you
        here, all present ?

[12]

down the corridor wound like a horn
and not a glimmer
                    to the first signs
half a mile in from the surface
you touch but don't believe,
nor shadow of a glimmer down beyond them
        your eyelids
                    jumping like fish
veil nothing here: you are the very
        shadow you discarded

            all is eyes

        your path
        a spiral groped along, past
cataracts of stalactite
        stalagmite screens, chasm
            waterfalls, chimneys, columns
                        and with a twist
        upwards through a manhole
                    sides worn smooth

into the gigantic halls
                    the
            know not where

Light,

   and your hands
   a sudden shielda torch
   shaking out shadows

         against a blaze of inner noon
         your blindness

you

   there, my
   sister ? my brother ?

pounding
of blood across temples

         breath
         an instant held

   the drip
   drip of distant water

that unfathomable roaring

where sleeps the man
who shaggy haired
   roamed the steppes
       with wolf and bison
    ate grass, and played
       with the herds

           in *that time*

  before she came
      with her ear-rings
of amber   her breasts bared
    her armpits scented
  let down her braided hair
and struck you with that gaze of stone
  taught you the art of her stone smile
     woke you with language
    of cattle
byre and cave

  I am awake
  sleeping, I wake

           in *that time*

  before Delilah

[14]

and where now

      brother of boyhood
   male half of my otherness
      strong as the beasts you hunted with
before we hunted

      how have I lost you
in this cave blackness   dancing
   blinded by a mask of hands
              in *that time*
      by my own cunning

      changed my face
      like one gone
         under sunlight
      or a long journey

aye we must treasure the dream whatever the sorrow

      brother, you
   were the axe at my side
      my hand's strength
      the sword in my belt

              in *that time*

  standing in this cave of light
     this mouth of stone
    that eats me

[15]

words you rush in on me like a surf
into my core like semen to the uterus
like torchlight on these stones
moving and melting the frost's shadow behind them
trebling their din with intervening silences

and who is this come riding
in on the foam this long haired
green creature who brings me
back again among the scattered seasons

once I was young enough to think
you like these stones were immortal

in the wave that gathers you up in it like a sandgrain
and drops you down somehow else,
                     has it changed you, the sea ?

has it turned you into a fish ? a note ? a pearlseed ?
in the silt did you taste like this ?
whose was it that kiss,
               who was it embraced you ?

        jetsam of dream,
        eroded

down in the pit I have seen your face   mother
    your skull in the rockface

        and who is that other
           face in shadow
           the cloud that lurks just behind you ?

[16]

stone
you too

a monad

atom
    as I am

what is the sum
of these quanta ?

        I am not just
        my body

are you
      stone
my body ?

the total ?

[17]

under my eyes   these stones
                are

            dancing

                stars

                    birds

        figures of speech

growing into each other
                out of each other

    and have become
the spaces   between them

                        points
                in the dance

            including me
            enclosing me

me, embraced
        in this dance of stone

stone in me
stone that I am
centre or periphery
nomad and society of atoms

    eyed by stone
    eaten by stone
    loved by stone

danced in the dance
      by the dance
      of stone

by stone
    uttered
by stone
    dreamed

bloody stone
   blood I am
grained
   with breath
death of ancestors
   of my blood
  stone I am

wizened

  enduring

    the sun's hammer
    the frost's nails
    the wind's arsenal

adamant

   defying discourse
     messages
eyes   tongues

   telling nothing
giving nothing
    being of absence
core   the dream

   threshold
    ledge of energy
meniscus of darkness
   grain of light

   bringing to life
in me what does not exist
me in what does not exist

       subversive stone

   uprooting
  word from language

winding down
  time to rubble

    this continuum

  in you

all is the saying

[21]

in my throat
the man rises
   from the cave he was immured in

       break
     speech
in a tide on these stones
        wash
clean   break
     word
into stone
   out of stone

          sleeping, I wake
          I am awake

   and the ghost gone at end
   of childhood

comes back
eroding, endures

  among these ancestors

       sharing

[22]

in the neat but functional lines
                    of Block H
in the beige walled waiting room
                    of The Labour Exchange
in the public bar of The Tiger
            or The Square and Compasses
in the new auditorium
        of The College of Arts and Technology
in the Maplan Supermarket
    that sells everything

            who rent out
        a plot of elements
            who lodge in
                seams of space
        with just room to move
            from corner to corner
        in a web of gravities
                thick as a word
            shimmering
        on a beam of time
                bound there
                    to say out

from what is between these hands
from what is under these eyes

                ancestors' fathers
        locked in stone
            we struggle out of
                measuring
            immeasurables

[23]

this was no whore
        not abandoned
not 'wild'
        and cruel only

    when an absence
and no gap
        between speech and her mouth

            matter of words
            word of matter

    always touch
lips touch
                    speech
tongues   the world
        born

                wherever

        light of eyes
        eye of light

child of elements

    wherever
            touch and find
anywhere centre

                    say these stones
                    of Avebury

[24]

find any
where centre

      echoes from peripheries
      out of galactic range

      creatures awake on distant shores
      across those seas and skies

      beyond sidereal thoughtspan back
      to breathing

           waves
           expanding, re-echoing

including
us here

enclosing
us here

      say the stones

now every
where centre

      I do not tell   *I say*

Great Shelford, 1971

31

Lightning Source UK Ltd.
Milton Keynes UK
UKHW03f1113200318
319744UK00002B/29/P